Facing the Elements

Nancy —
Thank you for bringing
your gifts to so many!
Paul

Facing the Elements

Poems

by Paul Friedrichs

BURNHAM
B
PRESS

Burnham Press, 9 Newfields Road, Exeter, N.H. 03833

To all my loved ones,
with special appreciation
for my wife Jane.

Winter

Spring

Winter

Hot Tub after a Long Day at the Hospital

Evening snowfall
gently blankets the
hurt
loss and depravity
encountered in one day's work
at the hospital
where young men turned old by bad choices
and old women turned frail by tobacco
sit in glass booths of gowned isolation
where babies with broken bones
from unprepared fathers
and unrevived grandmothers still on machines
despite prodigal feats
await their modern-world fate.

> But around this warm womb
> holding me naked
> under the night sky
> the snowy field lies silent
> and the powdered pine
> stands heroic and accepting,
> our backyard talisman
> quietly watching decades
> of human debris.

On Track

Sometimes it's nice
when the furnace is working
the roof is sound
and the windows are sealed
against the north wind
to go outside
in the fresh fallen snow
and watch ski tips
forge ahead
into white oblivion
while the crystalline cold
bites your cheeks
clouds your breath
and sends warm-blooded life
burrowing for survival
your parallel tracks
extend with intention
where they will take you
you do not know
for the glide is the thing
striding into the moment
finding your rhythm
in sap-arresting air
comforted by knowing
a warm fire awaits you
and your venture out
into this forbidding world
is a choice
that can be remedied
by a cup of hot chocolate.

93

some kind of lonely
to have outlived friends
and spouses and take
each day because it's
served to you
stiff in the hips and
everywhere else slowly
urinating unless it leaks
first
how graceful one must be
to accept the last straw
still reading the obits to
make sure you're not
there

Northern Exposure

Climbing a mountain without you
my sole seeks foothold
in time-weathered rock
dressed grey-green with lichen.
The cold brings a taste
of bitter nights to come
as we strive on, father and son,
to the warmth-depleted mountaintop.

The first snow has fallen,
slickening the hill
and cautioning my step
which yet loosens a stone
to join other slough
in the gully below.
Clammy sweat collects under my anorak:
warm in the toes, cold in the heart,
when will lonely feel good?

Fully exposed at the peak
we descend to sheltered elevation
among the anonymity of tree and forest
where the fresh snow mixes
with bright autumn colors.
Placing foot in front of foot
we obligingly march on
and in the now settled terrain
my son (who has announced
he is too grown to be kissed)
places his gloved hand in mine.

Snowstorm

Hush now child
and calmly receive
my accumulating blanket;
seek shelter and simply watch
as I powder your world
into new landscape
which muffles your murmurings
of civilization.
Become grateful for fur
and edible roots in hibernation
as I take my time
quieting your ambition.
Set aside lists
and imperatives
and pause before your window
to realize you have
nothing to do, really,
but put on your skis.

Departed

Empty casings hold the stillness
of spent time, musty vapors
of afterthought and once-was.
Now pain travels elsewhere
like a train leaving the station.
As each unwilled breath
draws us down the track
we are sidecars receiving
the unsought gift of new scenery,
pistoning past regret to just-is.

Somewhere there's a field
of daisies reaching for the sun,
a stream rippling over rocks,
an ocean waving towards the shore
and a heart that beats on.

The Fact Is

The fact is I love you:
even on days when I need to
wrap the scarf a little tighter
while I wait for the radiator to clank on,
even when your quietness does not include me,
even when my touch turns you cold.
Your belly is pleated with maternity,
your arches fallen among arthritic toes,
your hair turning silver,
but goodness within you rises
to the top like cream
and your soul knows how to fly.
In joining you, I too have wings.

Facing the Elements

Over the Mountain
top down under winter-grey skies
my engine pulls me
8 degrees Fahrenheit through Crawford Notch

I'm alone save cold pavement
drifting snow flakes
and a crow eating road kill
as Paul Simon sings
"Nowhere to hide, Nowhere to hide…"

Somewhere a skier slides
a frozen branch snaps
an icicle breaks free
as up the gorge my body heat dissipates
just a whisper to Old Man Winter

SIDS

Gone is the smile that fed our souls,
the clean drool from soft gums,
the warm snuggle under mama's chin
and the sound of her breathing
reminding us why we're alive.

Hope falls from our chests
like a greased lead pipe
into a fathomless pit.
How can we revive our own breath
and coax our own stuttering hearts to beat on?

We remember her fine blond hair,
vanilla-powder skin,
delicate grip
and the quietness with which she slipped
from our grasp into timelessness.

Mi Solar

O sol of my soul,
   you bring me absolution;
Can anything not be undone
   by the warmth of the Mexican sun?

Light

Light pierces darkness,
bathes innocence,
bestows warmth and
awakens life
where quiet has been.
It resounds,
yet carries its own silence.
It defines worlds,
softens faces,
exposes evil.
Light beckons,
carries hope,
comforts
and guides us home.

Lost

Falling naked
into the vortex of
anti-matter
spread-eagle before eternity
bewildered beyond consciousness
I wake to hear you breathing
and reach out
to find you sleeping next to me.

Red Bird in Winter

The cardinal loops to the tree
on the far side of the field
and sits in bare branches
aware of its brilliance
against grey and white landscape,
content to be the sole totem
on a cold winter's day
of warmth and hope
awaiting the return of
thaw and bud.

Crossing the River

Running the beach alone
I pause to cross the sluice
on stepping stones,
each one a short-lived refuge
in the passing torrent.
Some are firm, some are tippy,
and on this cold day
some are slippery with ice.
Impertinent to the squawking gulls
or the thumping waves
I halt midway, daunted
by the risk of passage,
yet needing new terrain
I leap ahead
to a rock slicker than the last,
and stare dumbfounded
as my foot vanishes
into cold and wet.

Now baptized and impatient with caution,
I'm to the other side in three leaps more:
firm ground, a new pace,
my sock and running shoe
squeezing out the slop
as I find my rhythm again.

Spring

Mud Season

Leaving crystal chandeliers at the Grand Hotel
we descend wooden stairs crusted in salt
and cross the old bridge whose white paint
began peeling years ago.

Back to our real lives
I caress you one last time
as the White Mountain Forest glides by
in the afternoon light.

Grey snow melts by the wayside
and we pass under rusting bridges
in silence, measuring our regret
without remorse,

coming home with soles
tracking inconvenient prints,
messy but necessary
for spring.

Earth Skin

Our membrane of life-sustaining
atmosphere
resilient yet vulnerable

you have the power
to melt meteors and
kick up hurricanes
which snap bridges like toothpicks

a living organism
on which we depend
you breathe our protection yet
we have not honored you
in our race for combustive consumption

rather we taunt and degrade you
and denude the skin we need
while claiming entitlement
to all of God's work.

> May we quiet our ambition
> and work together in sustenance
> so as not to travel raw
> through this mighty universe.

To Kathy on March 5, 2012

Like a bird on the wing
glancing moments are gone
in a flash almost lost
before they're remembered,
incomprehensibly drained
now unfairly arrived,
trapped in bewilderment
once here but not now.

In that pause
when the breeze stops
the world must decide
when to inhale again
with a sigh then a whimper
nature creaks on its axle
of quotidian change
leaving one truth behind:
    To have never lost
     is to have never loved.

The Last Day of March

Ice floats down the river
crocuses bloom
a tulip pierces the soil
and as I trim the lavender
a groundhog explores the damp field.

Open your eyes to beauty
and germination
and sunlight
and everyday growth.
The breeze moves stems
unable to move themselves
and ants traverse petals
content with their horizon.

The Killing

The sharp-eyed gliding bird
dives abruptly
on the small rustle
of moving fur
caught midstride
in strong talons.

Somewhere a mother's heart
stutters a beat
while elsewhere
a hatchling's digestion stirs.

Suicidal Ideation

Riding the train with strangers
down track cut like a gash
through the concrete city
we take you to the County hospital
named for a king worlds away
from your present misery.
I long to hold you
my beloved child
and place you back in your cradle
but now you are old enough
to drift free and own life's pain,
broken promises and uncertainty.
As the morning light flickers
on the colorful graffiti
and spring bloom passing by
I only wish for you again
to feel the sunshine, smell the flowers
and taste the innocence
of this new unbroken day.

(Being in) The Present

Each day is like a bubble
    blown from soapy water
        through a small plastic hoop
Drifting away in shifting air
    delicate, formed,
        complete for a moment
then gone out of sight
    or popped with a splash.

Others follow-- float, pop, float, pop
    each with its moment of perfection
        timeless for one second
Not mourned because
    there are more to come,
        until there are no more...
But the world rests cleaner,
    shinier,
        soapier for their presence.

I Like

The taste of fresh cut apples
  that spray as you bite
the familiar fit of our fingers
  as my hand slides into yours
the smoothness that feels new
  each time I enter you
the smell of our hayfield
  warm with sunshine in May.

Full Moon Rising

Look!
Above the tree tops it comes
Full
Reflective
Relentlessly rising

How powerful it seems,
Hopeful
Awesome
Transcendent
Feminine and complementary
to its celestial partner,
without whom
it wanes into shadow.
Coupled,
it illuminates our world
and remedies the darkness.

Well Being

My wholeness like a peach
feels vulnerable
to the moods of time
its fingered flesh
is easily bruised
an impatient bite
finds firm unwelcome
and inattention is rewarded with decay
but when the moment's right
my trust lies open
and my joy yields such sweet juice
all I can do is swallow.

Homecoming

Like wileful littermates
we circle the bar
in the balloon-filled gymnasium,
biding how-are-you's
and remember-when's
until breath-stiffening, pulse-quickening
I find your blue-eyed smile
framed by unfamiliar wrinkles,
long hair still curled
and discreet cleavage bolstered
by a few extra pounds
you stand erect and proud
with a resilience honed
by years of disappointment.
We greet warmly
and exchange pleasantries
and think
about what might have been,
sharing a final embrace
before parting
with a touch
of regret.

Abigail

Dear One,
from whence did your spirit arise?
"My father is Joy" you told me
and you brought me joy,
a world of creativity
and three wonderful children

Such determination to love
through sadness and pain
you forgave me and others
who hurt you
and I loved you enough
to be hurt by you, too
and feared losing you so
that I took the wrong path.

Now you rest in shadow
and swim with the dolphins
and leave us your gentleness
as we look forward
to hearing you sing again.

The Miracle of the Monarchs

You the great traveler
and the great transformer,
you know what is right.
The sun tells you it is time
and earth's magnetism guides you,
you know not where
but it is right.
In the cool of the mountain you sleep,
in the sun you come alive
and outlive your parents eightfold
before starting the journey again,
just a bug with the will of a giant,
because God said so.

Summer

Vacation Checklist

First order of business
  catch up on your sleep
  watch your weight, a little
  but spend a little money
  to prove you're having fun
  feed the ducks,
  buy some beer
  read a book you wouldn't have
  and don't get too much sun
  let go of your tomorrow
  catch a bird with your binoculars
  no regrets from living yesterday
  and find a pretty shell
  no ice cream headaches
  no sand between the sheets
  start the day with an adventure
  and end it loving well.

Men and Boys

That summer Bruce and I
each packed a bag
and made a road trip
to see the boys
living off salsa and sandwiches
at their summer digs.

Discarding our neckties
and pocketing keys
for a trip on the ferry,
back to an age
of fun and simplicity,
beer pong and bike rides,
we jumped off the bridge rail
into salt water
born again to the passage
and rituals of youth.

Initiates in fraternity
we rose to the occasion
in the gauntlet of games,
demonstrating we too can be boys,
and they can in loving us be men.

Seawater, Martha's Vineyard

Mother's embrace of smooth salinity
buoyant offering from an ancient world
conveying me back to an endless childhood
fragrant with mollusk and kelp.

Serenaded by ruffling waves on the shore
I float like a turtle with limbs astride
my shadow vanishing in green-glass below
releasing my shore-bound woes.

The hum of a motorboat somewhere unseen
incessant tocsin of new world order
cannot steal me from my absolution
in this, God's primordial broth.

The Outsider

Is there a reason for a single blade of grass
to stand above the lavender?
It collects light like any other, and did not ask
to grow alone and face the ire
of an exacting gardener.
Does it feel abandoned, or simply fortunate
to seek the sun in isolation,
to breathe the air for a few days
or a few weeks before it is discovered,
pulled from its roots and discarded
to compost another season
of frenzied proliferation.
Will its parents mourn its passing?
Will its progeny return next year
to try again?
    Now shoulder to shoulder
    the lavender mumbles in satisfaction.

Mexican Cathedral

Sweep, sweep through the ages
sound and light filter
into the stone basilica
where old women witnesses
to human suffering
sit sparingly in plain wooden pews.
A breeze ruffles the altar cloth
while power tools and car horns
proceed in the distance.
Sweep, sweep, the street cleaners
clear the courtyard
as the virgin mother sits placidly
amidst the gilt of conquerors
and in the silent echo of time
her minions hold
the ache of generations.

Las Montanas

Quiet power now
once molten core
you rest in the sun or
part the clouds
while human stories cling
to your slopes like firs
or fall away like harvested timber.
Pueblo Madonna and child
appear ghostlike at your shoulder
while her people hover like bees
over the dry earth
and wait for the rain.

Seashells

Hard husks
of missing mollusk
you roll ashore as
spent carcasses
striving for the light
unperturbed by the waves
your birdpecked abodes
now sunbleached and forlorn
are marveled at by children
and other thin-skinned species
aged enough to admire
the permanence
you forged with stubborn insistence
that soft and simple lives
should not be soon forgot.

Foot Prints

Side by side
we pad the sand
letting incessant waves
be our conversation

our traverse proven
by a trail of imprints
which like the moment
will not last

but be washed clear
by morning when, freshly
we must declare
ourselves once more.

Father's Day 2007

My Gratitude feels like
clean sheets
at the end of a dog-tired day,
It looks like a tall pine
reaching for the sun from sandy soil,
and tastes like strawberry rhubarb pie
on a picnic with an ocean breeze.
My Gratitude smells like
your clean hair
when you hold me genuinely,
and sounds like my children's banter
as they joyfully engage life.

Venezia

How I long for
coming home
in water light
to sundrenched islands
in lagoon haven
safe on stilts in the mud
built stone after careful stone
into irrigated palaces
held in a flagstone maze
fed by ships trading silk and spice
where gondolas feather
under small bridges
in tight spaces
busy with life.

The Gondola

Everything truly important
fits into this gilded time capsule
that glides us between palaces
on hidden canals,
protected from tides
and swaddled against time
we float majestic in our sequester
unburdened by worries
from the wheeled world.

Summer People

When all is quiet on the water,
that hour after sunset
when the day seems on pause,
the rumble of ferry engines
fills the silence.

Gone are the smiling tourists
posing for snapshots
holding fried food and melting ice cream,
yet to come are the
slamming porch doors and laughter
ringing out in the dark.

How easily these days slide by
like the lapping of the waves.
All too soon the lighthouse speaks silently
but says it all:
with the blink of an eye
a day, a summer, a lifetime is gone.

Georgetown, Maine

Deer bound into the woods
as day breaks in foggy light
ferns drip with morning dew
still come the waves.

Heron nestle in the marsh
crabs scuttle pond to pond
sand collects between the toes
still come the waves.

Berries ripen in the sun
bodies falter as we age
gulls circle round the rocks
still come the waves.

Osprey search for their next meal
peace eludes our hungry souls
uncertain futures, unmet needs
still come the waves.

Storms pass with thunder booms
love's blanket calms the night
we awaken in resolve
still come the waves.

Letting go of old repose
driftwood left upon the beach
finding love will heal the day
still come the waves.

This Meadow – August 23, 2014

Life steps into this meadow
after river ice melt
birthing peepers then crickets
in vernal assault
spilling daisies and lilies
then fireflies that pop
before mice and mosquitoes
join the midsummer feast

in tall grass crowned by goldenrod
and royal Queen's lace
with milkweed prepared
for its downy release
we gather, pollinated families
in this sanctified field
over the fat gopher's lair
summer's promise fulfilled

after mist clears the river
under the osprey's keen gaze
while dragonflies hover
and butterflies flutter
the marsh grass dances
in the afternoon breeze
til the red fox pauses
in the spotlight of sunset

recalling the chill
of late August nights
we watch changing tides
roll towards winter
like the quick-footed chipmunk
stealing seed to his den
we're prepared by this bounty
for the lean times to come.

Fall

Spent Summers

On its hidden shelf
the brass key gathers dust,
a shaft of autumn-angled sun
spotlights flowers dried on their stalks,
and yellowed leaves scatter the path
trod by stiffened sandals
over long-cold sand.
Folded beach umbrellas
join mold-marked canvas chairs
in cobwebbed corners of the shed
where the clock, whose battery
is dead til Spring, stands still.

When I Cease to Be

When I cease to be
the waves will still roll to the shore,
the sun will still shine
and somewhere a squirrel will still climb a tree.
A breeze will stir the grass,
someone will take flight
and a kiss will heal.
My soul will be quiet,
my heart forever hold love,
and nothing will be beyond my reach.

Ebb Tide in Autumn

Dried sticks float wanly into
cold waters
as birds hurry south in search of
vanishing sun.
Long shadows mark
inevitable loss
as seasons age, years vanish
in golden glow of leaf and bleeding ivy.

Ripening pumpkins
defy the first fated frost
until their expiring flesh also
yields to mold
among drying stalks
awaiting the clean blanket
of winter's first snow.

Black Hole

Approaching the end
of my time on this spaceship
we call life
I crawl through the hatch
into a black void
to discover
actually
there are millions and millions
of stars out there.

Humanity

Here we are
outstretched
holding hands
a lacework of humanity
falling together as if
skydiving without parachutes
hooked together like
a Barrel of Monkeys
on this small vessel
we call Earth
all members of the same tribe
a genetic chain
fellow Humans
with the same velocity
falling fast
as opportunity
rushes past

Mr. Oak

I walk in awe
under your tortured branches
which spell a history
of gravity-defying ambition,
each weathered year a ring beneath your belt.
Ungentle wind and rain
have bent your limbs in knotty-elbowed dance,
as you strove for nothing more
than tranquil air and gracious sunlight
from unthirsty roots.

Do you feel pain within your substance?
Do you regret lost limbs,
or time after time leaving your bloom
to the forest floor?
You have marked more winters
than my grandfather's grandfather
with dignity and grace,
elegantly balancing as you do
the pull of the earth and the call of the sky.

The Real Olympics

Why do we pay such attention
to what teens and twenty-somethings
can do with their bodies?
Why don't we examine
the true endurance
of human endeavor,
what as forty-somethings we have done
with our hearts,
if as sixty-somethings we have
no regrets,
if as eighty-somethings we are
ready to leave?

Done

When the cows have come home
when the fat lady's sung
each grandchild's been born
and each wedding bell rung

the dishwasher's emptied
the last spoon put away
you've stumbled to bed
and called it a day

you've finished the laundry
and mopped up the floor
attended the wakes
and prayed for no more

you may now cross the river
the bridge is complete
there are no more regrets
just old loves to meet

when change in the weather
is no longer news
take the plunge, close the door,
cross the bridge.

Infirmary

(or Chemotherapy Blues)

Trepidation
wired to catheter restraints,
gut-wrenching acceptance
        of red toxin
flowing into accommodating veins
Calm demeanor over bridled terror
Loss is gain.

Redirected lives simmer
        in the antiseptic wait
        on borrowed time
Who is next to die?
Cautious glances cloak
        forced determination
Live, Live, fly away!

When sustenance
is hospital food on trays
we are broken birds
suffering the slow drain
        of vibrant lives
splinted for another spring
Navigating
        on Hope.

Marriage

Marriage
like a meadow
has its seasons
and is always best plowed
after a light rain

Soul Mate

Even closed
your eyes meet mine
and talk
as we lay entwined
in sleep.

My Favorite Part of the Day

My favorite part of the day
is waking next to you
gently snoring
restless dreams behind you
one arm raised above your head
in acceptance of a new day
together

Flight Check

Still in meditation
the jolt of turbulence
catches as we descend
through the clouds
and I awaken as if
from a dream in the heavens
my eyes still patched
I hear piano music
in my headsets
and feel suddenly I too
could play two-handed, syncopated
with both halves of my being,
the left and the right,
conscious and pre-conscious,
yin and yang,
knowing both sides of a fluent truth.

Pasaje de la Vida

It's a one-way street
where the jacaranda petals
settle each spring
on the cobblestones
where the clop of hooves
became the rattle of wheels
became the rumble of tires
with each new generation
quieted by funeral processions
and reborn in festival
where a father walks
his blue-smocked sons to school
and a grandmother still watches
from her window
above the fruit stand.

Self-Compassion

I like my ugly body,
my paunch, my hairy ear lobes,
my tight hamstrings
and varicosities,
my flatulence and hunger pangs
for it bears me through each day
to be in relationship
with this world, this sunrise,
this kiss, this breeze,
this flight of birds
alighting in the wilderness

*Paul Friedrichs is a family doctor
and lives with his family in Exeter, NH.*

Side by side
we pull the sled

CPSIA information can be obtained
at www.ICGtesting.com
Printed in the USA
FFOW03n2234080415
12435FF